A SINGLE ROSE

Godly Advice For Single Girls

HANNAH L M

Kindle Direct Publishing

Copyright © 2019 by Hannah L M

All rights reserved.

No part of this book may be reproduced in any form or by any electronic or mechanical means, including information storage and retrieval systems, without written permission from the author, except for the use of brief quotations in a book review.

IBSN: 9781096340379

Scripture quotations marked (NIV) are taken from the Holy Bible, New International Version®, NIV®. Copyright © 1973, 1978, 1984, 2011 by Biblica, Inc.™ Used by permission of Zondervan. All rights reserved worldwide. www.zondervan.com The "NIV" and "New International Version" are trademarks registered in the United States Patent and Trademark Office by Biblica, Inc.™

Scripture taken from the New King James Version®. Copyright © 1982 by Thomas Nelson. Used by permission. All rights reserved.

Scripture quotations marked (NLT) are taken from the Holy Bible, New Living Translation, copyright ©1996, 2004, 2015 by Tyndale House Foundation. Used by permission of Tyndale House Publishers, Inc., Carol Stream, Illinois 60188. All rights reserved.

Scripture quotations taken from the Amplified® Bible (AMPC),

Copyright © 1954, 1958, 1962, 1964, 1965, 1987 by The Lockman Foundation

Used by permission. www.Lockman.org

Cover Design: Hannah L.M.

Cover Image By: Annie Spratt, Unsplash

❀ Created with Vellum

CONTENTS

Introduction	v
1. Dealing with Loneliness	1
2. Trust Him	5
3. Come to the Lord	12
4. Complete in Him	15
5. Beautiful, Noble, Honorable	18
6. Use This Season Wisely	22
7. Never Settle	25
8. Dealing with Ex's	31
9. Dealing with Breakdowns	35
10. Feeling Desperate	39
11. The Question	45
12. Waiting For The Right Time	49
13. Preparing For The Future	54
14. Breaking Barriers	60
15. How You Think About Singleness	65
16. He Hasn't Forgotten You	72
17. Why Am I Still Single?	78
18. Asking Jesus Exciting Questions	85
19. Why A Single Rose Is Beautiful	89
Epilogue	92
Afterword	95
Notes	97
Also by Hannah L M	101

Introduction

In a world that is constantly shifting and rejecting truth, it's a challenge to stay pure. It's a challenge to patiently wait on the Lord. Remember you are not alone, there are many other ladies going through this season. I encourage you to always pray for them, even the ones you haven't met.

While I had hoped to be married by now, I have learned it's best to trust God and His timing. This doesn't mean it's always an easy thing to do, but I've learned a lot along the way. I am sharing with you some of what God has taught and shown me on this journey. My hope is that it will help you through the tough seasons of being single and, most importantly, to grow in your relationship with God.

Dealing with Loneliness

Jesus knows what it's like to be truly alone. His time in solitude went far beyond what we experience. He was abandoned by His closest friends during the most painful time in His life. Yet He never gave into loneliness;

> "A time is coming and in fact has come when you will be scattered, each to your own home. You will leave me all alone. *Yet I am not alone, for my Father is with me*" (John 16:32, NIV, Emphasis mine).

The last part of this verse is something we should memorize and teach ourselves to say, even when we are not lonely. Jesus knew He was never alone. He took a negative circumstance (His friends scattering) and replaced it with a positive (the Father being with Him). He did this before a lonely thought could get into His mind in. Surely if Jesus can say this in confidence before He went to the cross, we can follow His example.

It is clear that Jesus understood one of the main keys to overcoming loneliness; developing a strong, loving, and authentic relationship with our Father. We all ultimately have to do our Christian journey alone. While we may have friends and family to encourage and guide us, there will be times when they aren't physically with us. There will be other moments when we feel absent from them, even in their presence. During these times, remember the Father is with you.

Being single can have its share of lonely days. Open up to Jesus and tell Him how you're feeling. Instead of viewing singleness as something solitary, use it as a connection point to Jesus and others. During His time here on earth, Jesus was single, and you are also single, for the time being. When two people have something in common they often build a connection with each other. Have you ever considered asking Jesus how He felt about being single and how He dealt with it? I think sometimes we may be afraid to try and connect with the Lord about such personal feelings and issues. We need to remember that Jesus lived on this earth as a person and can sympathize with us.

> "For we do not have a High Priest who cannot sympathize with our weaknesses, but was in all *points* tempted as *we are, yet* without sin. Let us therefore come boldly to the throne of grace, that we may obtain mercy and find grace to help in time of need"(Hebrews 4:15-16, NKJV).

GRACE

I believe one way Jesus dealt with the tough seasons of singleness was by asking for God's grace. While we may hear the word a lot, and know it's something good, we often don't realize that grace is God's power. When we ask for His grace, He gives us His power and strength in place of ours.

> "But he said to me, 'My grace is sufficient for you, for my power is made perfect in weakness.' Therefore I will boast all the more gladly about my weaknesses, so that Christ's power may rest on me"(2 Corinthians 12:9, NIV).

Jesus is saying that His grace is not only enough for you, but that it's also made complete in your weakness. The Greek word used here for *weakness* implies weakness of the soul. If we choose to let it, being single can leave our souls feeling frail, so naturally we try to find someone or something to fix that. In 2 Corinthians, Jesus makes it clear that in our must vulnerable flaws, the weakest areas of our soul, His power is made complete.

The Greek word for *power* used in this verse is *dýnamis,* and is very similar to the English word used for dynamite.[1] I like to think of Jesus's power being explosive. God's explosive power is made complete in our areas of frailty and weakness, including the hard times of being single. While Jesus freely offers grace, I believe humbling ourselves, admitting our need, and offering them to Him are important steps to receiving his help.

PAUL CONTINUES on in verse nine saying that he will "most gladly" boast in his weakness, frailty, and sufferings. At times this statement is difficult to understand, let alone do. It's not always easy admitting we have weaknesses and then relying on Jesus to make them into something better. Paul has a point though, a very good one.

He goes onto say, "so that Christ's power may rest upon me". The word *rest* in Greek means "to raise a tent or tabernacle over, dwell".[2] Paul is excited because he understands that only in his weakest and most dreaded periods of life can Christ's power, might and strength, come to dwell on him.

Why should you be glad and thankful for lonely weeknights and the temptation to be envious over a friend's engagement ring? Because when you are weak, then can you be made strong. During these moments Jesus' strength can come dwell on you.

This is a process that takes time. While studying this verse, I came across an illustration given in the concordance of a pirate's telescope.[3] Imagine yourself opening an old telescope, one twist at a time, until, finally, when you look through the lens, the scope has reached its full capacity and effectiveness. While dealing with the lonely times of being single, keep asking God for grace, and over time you will grow stronger.

Dear Jesus,

Please give me Your grace to deal with this season of singleness. Give me grace to deal with the times I feel lonely, and help me not turn it into self pity. May You please forgive me every time I've complained or been negative about being single. Turn this season into something beautiful. I hand the loneliness and this period over to You now so that You can use it.

On the days I am hurting or feeling weak, give me strength and remind me to stay positive. Come dwell on my places of weakness so I can be strong in You.

Trust Him

Jesus knows that trusting is not easy for everyone. We each grow up in different circumstances that can determine how and who we choose to trust. Perhaps people from your past have hurt you, maybe intentionally, and they lack remorse for it. Trust is a hard thing to do when we've been wounded. Wounds distort our idea of trust and even when we desperately want to rely on God and others, we don't know how. Some of you, like me, have been so far removed from the word that you aren't even familiar with what it feels like.

Trust is extremely important for a relationship to be healthy, that includes your relationship with God and your future spouse. That's why healing from your past and learning to trust should be sorted out *before* you get married. If you don't know where to begin, try studying the definition of the word *trust;*

> "a firm belief in the reliability, truth, ability, or strength of someone or something".[1]

In order to move on to trusting your future husband, you must first learn to trust the Lord. Practice trusting that He is reliable and dependable. Trust in the truth of His words. Remember His ability and strength. He parted an entire sea in half, walked across the surface of water, and stopped in the middle of a noisy crowd to answer a blind man's call. The Lord is always available to listen and help us.

Trusting God

Many of us our familiar with Provers 3:5, but lets take a deeper look.

> "Trust in the Lord with all your heart, and lean not on your own understanding"(NKJV).

The word "trust" in the Hebrew text can also be translated, "Careless, confident, fall down."[2] Think about the images these words create. If you trust someone, you are careless around them. You trust them so much you let your guard down around them. Imagine that you are participating in a trust exercise where you are required to fall down into someones arms. Instead of a person, practice this with the Lord, trusting Him enough to catch you.

Being confident in someone is a lot like trusting a good doctor. You believe the doctor you are seeing is well trained and knows what they are doing. You believe that they will do everything in their power to help you, not hurt you. It's similar to leaning on the Lord instead of ourselves. He knows what He is doing, and He is for you, not against. The more you learn to trust God and what that feels like, the more you will realize there is nothing to worry about, including if you will ever get married. You can move through life being single with confidence, feeling assured that Jesus knows what He is doing. His desires for you are always good.

What does it look like to trust the Lord with all of your Heart? The answer may look different for each of us, but God has not left us without direction. In the Hebrew text, the word "heart" used in Proverbs 3:5 has multiple meanings,*"the inner man, soul, comprehending mind, affections and will."*[3] Each of these words have a different context and effects us on different levels. Understanding each part will help you trust God more as a whole.

Your Inner Man

Inner man is not a phrase we use today, but I feel it means our inner being. This includes everything that is not related to our outward physical self. Your inner being is everything that makes up you, including your mind, affections, spirit and soul. In 1 Samuel 16:7, the Lord sends the prophet to anoint a new king for Israel. After seeing all of Jesse's son's not one was found to be God's chosen, despite their dashing appearances. God made it clear to Samuel that He does not look at the outward appearance, as man does, but at the heart. The word used for heart in Samuel is the same word used in Proverbs 3:5. God is looking at our inner being, and He tells us to love him with all of it.

Your Soul

The deepest thing you can trust someone with is your soul. Trusting anyone on this level often requires a step of faith. Sometimes it's not just a small ordinary step, but a step like Peter took when he put his foot out of the boat and onto the water. Imagine the type of relationship required for Peter to know Jesus so intimately that he felt secure enough to walk on top of water during a raging storm. The trust needed to make that type of move is not found on the surface, but deeply in our souls. It's clear what happened when Peter took his eyes off the Lord, it destroyed his trust and the waters began to take him down. I feel trusting God with your soul is a deep connection that grows over time. It can't be achieved with shallowness, but with diligent studying, obeying, and seeking of the Lord.

Your Mind

Trusting the Lord with your mind involves renewing your mind. If you are listening to thoughts from the enemy that are doubting Jesus, or making you feel anxious about your future, you are not trusting the Lord with your mind. A renewed mind catches those thoughts before they can even take root and throws them out. A Godly mind also takes time to create trusting thoughts and purposely thinks on them, as well as memorize scripture.

Your Affections

Trust the Lord with all of your affections. I feel affections are physical expressions of love or feelings. If you have been hurt by people you've given your affections to, it can be a challenge to place them on the Lord. No matter your past, the truth is that Jesus is the safest place to put them. The Lord will never disregard, reject, or misuse any affections we give Him. I believe He actually cherishes them. If you are unsure what it means to place your affections on the Lord, here are a few examples and suggestions;

- Write out a love letter to the Lord telling Him

what you enjoy most about Him, instead of fixating and pouring your soul out to a guy.
- Wake up early, or stay up late, to spend time talking with God.
- Instead of looking at your phone or texting someone first thing when you wake up, spend a few minutes thinking about God.
- Practice keeping your feelings and emotions in check when you "like" a guy or even when you are overly excited about something. Make sure your affections aren't surpassing the affections you have for the Lord. Everyone is human, so if you feel you're having trouble ask God for help.

Your Will

We often think of will power when we hear this word, but I feel it's another way of saying our desires. Do you trust the Lord with your deepest desires? For example, lets say you have a strong desire to travel the world. At this moment, it's not an option for you, which most days is just plain frustrating. You feel those desires to travel are there for a reason, but can't understand why God would not allow you to fulfill them. Instead of getting upset, or forcing things to go your own way (IE planning a spur of the moment trip to Ireland) trust that God has a plan.

It's likely He's the one who put it there and there's a purpose for it in the future. Many of us have a strong desire for a family and a husband, but for now those desires are not being fulfilled. That doesn't mean God made a mistake, or that He won't fulfill those desires. It does mean that we need to entrust each of these desires into the Lord's hands, so he can fulfill them in His good timing.

I'm sure many of you have had difficult pasts. It can feel exhausting trying to gain the strength to put what little trust you have on the Lord. We have to remind ourselves that He is trustworthy and worth the effort. So we could be made whole, Jesus voluntarily chose this;

> "But He was pierced for our rebellion, crushed for our sins. He was beaten so we could be whole. He was whipped so we could be healed. All of us, like sheep, have strayed away. We have left God's paths to follow our own. Yet the Lord laid on Him the sins of us all" (Isaiah 53:5-6, NIV).

Keep in mind how deeply Jesus loves you as you grow to trust in Him.

Try it:

- Don't put God in a "I can't trust you box" because it hurts Him, and you. Apologize and ask for His forgiveness. Ask Him to teach you how to trust Him.
- Developing trust in God will also help you prepare for marriage by allowing you to trust your future spouse. Pray for God to start developing trust between you and your spouse now, even if you have never met.
- Make a list of four or more times the Lord has been reliable or there for you. When you are having troubles trusting, look over them.

Dear Jesus,

May You please forgive me for all of the times I chose to not trust You. I struggle with understanding what it means to rely on You with all of myself. My past hasn't always taught me how to trust, sometimes I don't even know what it feels or looks like. I don't want to have a shallow trust in You. Please show and teach me to trust You and the good people You have put in my life. Destroy all of the enemies lies about trust, and forgive me for believing them, I'm sorry. Begin to build in me a trust strong enough to walk with You on water.

In Jesus name amen.

Come to the Lord

❦

"Come to me, all you who are weary and burdened,
and I will give you rest"(Matthew 11:28, NIV).

It's important to the Lord that you come to Him during the times when you're feeling frustrated about being single. Without His guidance and help, you risk turning to, self-pity, bitterness and jealousy. God cares about you. He knows your every thought, feeling, hope and dream. He knows everything about you, including that you would like to get married. 1 Peter 5 has a great verse that can remind you to throw your worries onto God.

"Therefore humble yourselves under the mighty hand
of God, that He may exalt you in due time..." (1
Peter 5:6 NKJV).

Notice the last part of verse six, in particular the word *exalt*. In Greek, it means to "raise or lift high".[1] When we choose to humble ourselves under God's mighty hand, our circumstances will change. Jesus will literally raise you high above your problems of singleness. Including worries, loneliness, discouragement, and mistrust.

There is more than one way to humble yourself. You can choose to be fully dependent on the Lord, dismissing reliance on yourself. You can also physically humble yourself by kneeling before Him, remembering that He is strong and powerful. I like to think on the definition given in the Greek text of God's majesty, "mighty-*dominating* (manifested) power, referring to God's supreme mastery (unrivaled dominion)."[2] Remembering His strength and ability will help us to humble ourselves and trust Him. It's also a great reminder that setting you up with a husband is no hard task for Him!

Verse 7 in 1 Peter goes on to say;

> "...casting all your care upon Him, for He cares for you" (1 Peter 5:7 NKJV).

In the Greek text, the word "all" means "whole, every kind of" and the word "cast" means "to place upon or throw".[3] Picture yourself taking each anxiety about your singleness, future and anything else bothering you, and placing them in the Lords hands (or throwing, whichever you prefer). In the last part of the verse, the word "care" in Greek means "to be concerned with, pay attention to, show interest".[4] It's touching to know that the Lord is actually concerned about our anxieties and worries. He is here for you and wants to hear about your worries.

TRY IT;

- Humble yourself before the Lord, and be willing

accept His plans and timing for you. If that is difficult, ask for His help and strength.
- Make a list of top five (or more) worries and struggles you have about being single, and getting married. Hand each worry over the Lord.
- When it gets tough, remind yourself that Jesus was single. He knows how it feels, and is here for you.

Dear Jesus,

I come to you today. Even if I am feeling content at the moment, I know there will be times when I don't. I know it says in Your word that You care for me, so I'm asking that You please help me during my season of being single. Help me humble myself before You and trust You with my future. Give me strength to turn away from being jealous and bitter. Remind me to hand each worry and fear about my future over to You.

Amen

Complete in Him

Sometimes we need to be reminded that we are searching for the wrong thing. Society, along with an array of movies and books, leads us to believe the lie that we are incomplete by ourselves. The world insinuates that if we find a boyfriend or a spouse, that will change. We often hear things like, *I found my soul mate, my other half, or my missing piece.* We're led to believe that once we attain this, we are then complete.

However, the reality portrayed in the romance world isn't truth. Always choose to evaluate those words and ideas compared to what the Lord says is true. The truth is, the only man who can complete you is Jesus. The "missing piece" is your heavenly Father, and you will only be whole in the Lord. At times it doesn't feel this way, and our souls long for something else to fill them, ideally a sweet guy, or a loving family of our own. As Christians, we are called to fight anything that sets itself up against God, including our own feelings.

Paul tells us to fight the good fight of faith. Faith is the opposite of doubting. Don't doubt God's goodness, His ability to fulfill you, His loving power to make you whole, and start using your faith. Fight the negative thoughts and feelings that try to creep into your mind and soul. Instead, rely and lean on the Lord.

Colossians 2:10 says;

> "and you are complete in Him, who is the head of all principality and power."

That means that Jesus completes you, not a boyfriend or a husband. He is also head over all power and authority, meaning He is able to fulfill you despite any evidence to the contrary.

A few years back I had a dream that illustrates this. I was standing around talking to some people, when, suddenly, Jesus came up and hugged me. As he hugged me, it was as if every broken, empty piece of my soul and self that felt hurt or incomplete, was filled. I felt whole, like I had finally found everything I had been searching for, and it was in Jesus. In the dream I didn't realize who was hugging me. When He pulled away from the hug I distinctly remember saying, "Who *are* you?!" and feeling like "Yes! That's what I've been longing to feel all along!"

TRY IT:

- Make a list of several things you feel you have tried or are trying to complete yourself with.
- Apologize to the Lord than hand each over to Him.
- Ask Jesus to help you better understand that only He can complete you.

Dear Lord,

I am sorry for trying to complete myself with things other than You. I'm sorry for seeking and trying to fill myself with things and people, when really I know deep down I should come to You. Sometimes it's an accident, and I don't mean to, but other times I just choose not to. Forgive me for both Lord, and please teach me not to do that, but instead fill myself with You. Point out to me when I try to use things to fill myself or when I turn to things I shouldn't. Show me what it means to be complete in You and lacking nothing. Even when this season gets lonely and tiresome, help me feel and be whole.

In Jesus name, Amen.

Beautiful, Noble, Honorable

"But I say this as a concession, not as a commandment. For I wish that all men were even as I myself. But each one has his own gift from God, one in this manner and another in that"(1 Corinthians 7:6-7, NKJV).

I the verse above, Paul is talking about remaining unmarried. He calls singleness a *gift*. I know that somedays this statement seems inconceivable, but I believe God inspired Paul to call it that for a reason. The important question to ask is why? I think the answer may be different for each person. Right now my singleness is a gift because I have more time to write. It allows me to fully prepare for the future and heal from my past, as well as spend valuable time with my family. Your singleness might be a gift because it allows you to do more things for the Lord, help people in need, or develop the special gifts He has given you.

If you find yourself struggling, review the last part of the verse;

BEAUTIFUL, NOBLE, HONORABLE

> Now to the unmarried and the widows I say: It is good for them to stay unmarried, as I do" (1 Corinthians 7:8, NKJV).

In particular, look at the word *good*. In the Greek text, it has multiple meanings but all of them are positive; beautiful, noble, and honorable are a few.[1] The word is defined as; *attractively good; good that inspires (motivates) others to embrace what is lovely (beautiful, praiseworthy)*."[2]

Soak in the positive attitude Paul has about being single. When we live single for God's purposes, it appears attractively good to others. In other words, it inspires, helps, and encourages them to embrace what is truly lovely in life.

Do you think about your time being single as inspirational and useful? Or what about admirable? Today it seems not many people are single. With the rise of social media, and relationships without marriage, many couples are living together at a younger age. As I grow older, it's a rare occasion when I meet someone who is single, and when I do I can't help but admire them. Of course it's hard to admire someone who is negative and sulky. Having a positive attitude, much like Paul, is necessary if you want to help people and set a good example.

PAUL GOES ONTO TO SAY, "I wish all men were even as myself-" meaning he wishes more men where single like him. It's an odd thing to say, wishing that all men where single. God has allowed me to be single for roughly six years now, and I'm in my late twenties. After much complaining, I feel I'm finally beginning to understand what Paul means.

While getting married is equally wonderful, it would be beneficial if more people spent time being single for the Lord. By this I mean preparing and working with the Lord for His purpose. Taking out more time to develop and train for His special plan for you. The amount of growth and opportunity to mature are experienced differently while single. As you get older things come into perspective more. You begin to see what is really important as well as what you need to change in yourself to be more like Jesus.

All of this can be accomplished while married, but more readily while single. There's nothing wrong with marrying young, especially if it's God's plan, but there is much to do and we live in difficult times. Postponing marriage and family may be a huge benefit. The Lord's plan is different for everyone though, follow His guidance and do what's best for you. Just remember that you are Christ's ambassador, use your time of being single to inspire and set a Godly example for others.

TRY IT;

- Write down three reasons why your singleness is a gift, then thank God for them and the opportunities you have while single.
- When the enemy comes around trying to get you down, remember those reasons and that your time being unmarried is for a purpose.
- Make a list of at least three lies that are pestering you, repent for believing them, and then hand them to the Lord.

Dear Lord,

Please teach and show me how being single can be a gift. Teach me to see it that way and as something beautiful, noble, and honorable. Show me how I can be a role model for others during this season, as well as how I may serve you. Help me grow during this time, becoming more like You and making changes You see fit. Teach me to start serving You now and working towards the plans You have designed for me to do.

In Jesus Name, Amen.

Use This Season Wisely

There are many people alive now who wish they had more time. Others regret how they've spent their past. Don't make the same mistake, choose to use your time with wisdom and the Lord's guidance. There are moments when we all struggle with this. It feels easier to waste hours on meaningless things when we are hurting or feeling alone. It comes more naturally to block out the pain then to come to the Lord or spend time with Him. Which when you stop to ponder it, is very unwise.

I wish someone would have told me what I'm about to tell you; now is the perfect season to develop a stronger relationship with Jesus. Carve out time in your schedule daily and purposely invest in your relationship with Him. Study the Bible, in depth, and practice learning how to pray. Ask the Lord to open your eyes to new things during this season. Ask Him to give you wisdom on how to spend your days and years. The enemy has created a world of distractions and things to keep us preoccupied. He wants us to think and dwell on anything but Jesus. It's definitely time to change that.

Invest in being healed, and preparing for the future. For each of us this will look differently. For myself, I struggle with wounds of rejection, fear, anger, and bitterness. All of those things need to go if I want to overcome and move forward in what the Lord has planned for me, including marriage.

While I don't know from personal experience, I have heard from married couples that marriage brings out things in us, good and bad. Living that closely with another person this is to be expected. The more you are healed now, the less likely you are to hurt your future spouse, kids, and yourself.

Our time here on earth is short. There is much to be done, and many who need our help. There are people you interact with daily that desperately need God. The smallest gesture, a smile, a compliment, can drive back the darkness someone is living in. Instead of dwelling on our feelings, as painful as they can be, dwell on pouring out what God gave you onto others. If you're a social person and great at talking, use your gift to uplift and encourage people or simply give them some company. If you're reserved and artsy, send someone a nice card or even a smile. Whatever your gift is, just get out and use it.

It's no secret that the future will hold dark times. Spend your single years preparing for the future, and the work the Lord has for you to do.

TRY IT:

- Sit down and either write out or mentally think about how you spend your time. Ask yourself, "Would Jesus be happy about how I'm spending my time?"
- Ask the Lord to show you areas where you should

be spending your time more wisely and practice adjusting how much time you spend on things like youtube and social media, as well as tv.
- Today, this week, and in general, keep your eye open for people who need help or encouragement. Ask the Holy Spirit to help you find people who are in need.

Dear Lord,

I know I don't always used my time wisely. I've wasted hours on useless things that bring You no glory and help no one. Please forgive me for wasting Your gift of time. Help me to see this season of being single as that, a gift. Open my eyes to areas where I am wasting time, but also let me know when it's okay to take a break. Help me spend this season of being single growing deeper with You and in what You have planned for me. On days where this feels tough, please give me Your grace.

In Jesus name, Amen.

Never Settle

I heard someone say once, "You get what you settle for." It's true, and during your journey, you may encounter an opportunity to settle for a guy that isn't God's best. If you settle for less, you will get less. If you wait for the Lord and His timing, you will get His best.

Part of the temptation in settling is that it can feel a lot like comfort. Like a guarantee that we've gotten what we've been waiting for. Settling for someone or something that is outside of God's will is dangerous. After all, if it's not God's desire and plan for you, whose is it? Chances are high that it is the enemies, and you giving in is part of his plan to hurt you.

I had a friend once who appeared, on the surface, to be someone I could consider dating. He claimed to be a Christian, was good looking, and we had a lot in common. We seemed to get along well and got together regularly for breakfast. Over time, he asked me if I would be interested in dating him. Truthfully I wanted to say yes, I thought about how our possible dating story would sound good, at least on the surface.

We met among mutual friends at a Bible study group, we both had the same job, shared our mutual love for animals, and even shared favorite movies. However, In my heart, without even stopping to ask the Lord, I knew he wasn't the person planned for me. I considered the idea of trying it out, after all it would be so *convenient*. We knew each other well, and dating wouldn't be that big of a step. Despite the positives, there where several, if not more, red flags that God revealed to me that I couldn't ignore. Later, after declining his invitation, I noticed that while he may have loved God, he didn't act like it.

Had I settled for those fleeting temptations that went as quickly as they came, very bad things would have happened. Most importantly I would have been outside of God's will, a dangerous place to be. When we are outside God's will we're an easy target for the devil. Little choices often lead to big consequences. Don't settle for convenience when you know it's not what God wants for you. The Lord loves you, and has a beautiful life and relationship planned for you, even if it doesn't appear so now. Choose to trust him.

Once, I was in my car ready to take my keys out and head in side, when the song playing caught my attention. I sat there for a moment and listened to the words, "It's not faith if you use your eyes."[1] Even though the Bible tells us to live by faith and not sight, hearing it that time struck me. How often do we use are physical eyes when Jesus has told us to use our faith? Stop using your eyes and mind to see the situations you're in, and look under the surface using your faith. The Lord will show you how He is working. Things will get clearer as you realize the Lord is always moving, even when our lives feel still.

With this in mind, be strong and fight the temptation to

settle for the wrong guy, or wrong anything. Don't do it, ever, period. Use your faith to see that God is creating a good future for you. What He has planned for you is special, unique, and worth the wait. You'll be so happy you trusted Him and His plan, you'll forget about how long it took to get there and the bumps along the way. Remind yourself that those who hope in the Lord will not be disappointed;

> "Then you will know that I am the Lord; those who hope in me will not be disappointed" (Isaiah 43:23 NIV).

SOUL TIES

God planned for two people to work alongside each other and develop a lasting relationship. He created sex to be more than just a physical bonding.

> " For this reason a man shall leave his father and mother and be joined to his wife, and the two shall become one flesh'; so then they are no longer two, but one flesh"(Mark 10:7-8, NKJV).

The word "joined" here means "to glue to, to glue in."[2] The Lord's idea for both sexual and emotional intimacy involves being so closely knit together, it's as if you are glued. You become one. When we attempt to create this type of bond with someone outside of marriage, our bodies and souls still mesh together. That's the way God designed it.

The problem with this, and modern dating, is that there's no lifelong commitment. You are not sealed in a marriage covenant. There's convenient opportunities for the relationship to end, which, when you've bonded so closely, is extremely painful. Your souls have started to grow together, and when you break up, they have to rip apart. It quite literally feels as if someone is being ripped from your soul.

There may be times when you feel it's so painful to break away from someone, it feels impossible. Sometimes, we even give in to temptation because the desire is so strong. No, you're not imagining it. Sex makes ending a relationship even harder because emotional and spiritual ties have been created. To start the process of breaking these connections, we need to repent openly to God and ask for His forgiveness.

IF YOU HAVE BEEN INTIMATELY INVOLVED with someone, it's important to cast out anything you may have picked up while your souls were bonding. When you have sex with someone, you are letting them into your "house" or temple. Your souls and bodies reach a level of closeness that can't be reached otherwise. While your bodies are connected, any issues or problems the other person has can be transferred over to you, and vice versa.

After repenting, and cutting any ties, you then need to cast out these issues. Ask Jesus to show you anything that needs to go. You might start by making a list of negative traits that person, or people, had. For example, if you know they struggled with anger and depression, cast those out of you. If you are unsure of where to start keep asking Jesus to help you.

Doing this will free your soul and help you heal. It will also insure that your future intimacy with the spouse God has planned for you will be pure. You will help eliminate the risks of transferring hurtful things to him, and be able to focus on developing your love instead of dealing with the past.

Ask the Lord to forgive you of every sexual and emotional bonding that happened outside of His will. After that, ask

Jesus to break each tie. You can also, using your faith, break them in the name of Jesus Christ. Doing this will significantly decrease the emotional pains from your past as well as cultivate healing.

Close bonds and ties can also be created between close friends and family as well.

> "Now when he had finished speaking to Saul, the soul of Jonathan was knit to the soul of David, and Jonathan loved him as his own soul" (1 Samuel 18:1, NKJV).

If you find yourself in agony over a friendship that has to end, try asking Jesus to cut the ties and bonding you have made. This will help you move forward and start new friendships while letting go of the past.

Try it:

- It's important to forgive each person who hurt you. If you refuse to forgive, the enemy's grip cannot be crushed. The Bible says God will not forgive us if we don't forgive others. If you feel this is impossible to do, be honest with Jesus and ask for His help.
- As mentioned, ask Jesus to forgive you and apologize for all and any type of sexual activity. It would be wise to make a list, as hard as that may be.
- Ask Jesus to break those ties and connections made on every level, physically, emotionally, spiritually, and mentally.

- Ask Jesus to help you cast out any traits or struggles that may have been transferred to you. If it helps, make another list. Cast each one out using your authority in Jesus Christ.
- Last, ask the Lord to give you strength not to settle!

Dear Jesus,

Please give me Your strength to never settle for less than Your best. Especially in the area of guys, but also in every part of my life. Sometimes I jump ahead of You and try to make choices out of impatience and mistrust. May You please forgive me. Help me be patient and remember that You're much wiser and Your ways much higher.

Lord, if I have crossed any lines, sexually, please forgive me. I ask You to please forgive me for each time and please cut any souls ties I have created that are not in Your will. Even if I haven't been sexually intimate, cut any ties I have made emotionally, physically, spiritually, and mentally that are not in line with Your desires for me. Any transfer spirits I have gotten from being intimate, please cast them out. Guide and continue to help me in this process. Help me heal. Thank You.

In Jesus name, amen.

Dealing with Ex's

The enemy usually tries to strike when we are weak. One way he may do this is by attempting to bring an ex back into your life. Let's say a close friend starts seriously dating someone and you're still single. Feelings start to rise in you that hurt, and you forget to trust the Lord. Next thing you know, you're reading a text message or listening to a voicemail from an ex who "just wanted to see how you were doing". Even worse, you may find yourself running into them at a store, where they are harder to ignore or avoid. If you stop to examine these situations, you'll see the enemy at work.

If, by chance, you're on good terms with the person, it may seem harmless just to say hi. The truth is that if this person is not living a Godly life, and you know the Lord does not want you around them, there is no reason for you to interact with them. Chances are high that you talking to your ex is a trap set up by the enemy. Ask God to give you the strength to turn away, delete the text, or ignore the phone call, even if it hurts. He knows what's best for you and has something much better planned for you.

It hurts God when we don't trust Him and instead choose to disobey. It is also disrespectful to your future spouse. Think about how you would react if you knew your future husband decided to re connect with an ex. You would feel upset, even if you haven't met yet. Choosing to be romantically involved with someone God does not want you around will only widen the gap between you and your future spouse. It will also create a gap in your relationship with God.Disobedience causes us to move backward, not forward. The Lord specifically tells us;

> "Forget the former things; do not dwell on the past. See, I am doing a new thing! Now it springs up; do you not perceive it"(Isaiah 43:18-19, NIV)?

There's a reason that the Lord tells us to keep our romantic feelings safely wrapped up until His timing has arrived. Bad experiences with people that we've dated can leave scars on our souls. These wounds in turn effect the rest of us, sometimes without us even knowing it. Thankfully, God gives us instructions on how to deal with them.

> "But I say to you who hear: Love your enemies, do good to those who hate you, bless those who curse you, and pray for those who spitefully use you" (Luke 6:27-28 NKJV).

Though the instructions are simple, forgive, bless, and pray, doing it is another thing entirely. When we start to take action by forgiving, sometimes our wounds get stirred up and festered. We are reminded why we dislike that person in the first place. The problem is that if these wounds aren't healed, we aren't healed.

In some circumstances the Lord may even choose to keep you single until you choose to forgive and release the pain to him. While I don't always understand Jesus's command to bless and pray for people who have hurt us, I do understand that He is God. If He says to do something, we should do it.

It helps to understand that people who are hurting, or have been hurt, often hurt others. Sometimes they do it on purpose, but other times they don't realize what they are doing. If a person has a rough past, and has not found God, how can we expect them to know how to treat others? They have no guidance, and the Lord is not living in them to direct them. This is not to say that their actions are justified, but it does mean we should try to see them through eyes of compassion. I have found that time helps with this, as well as praying to see them through Jesus' eyes.

TRY IT:

- Ask the Lord to protect you from any unhealthy relationships from you past, or present, including your Ex's. If you still have feelings for the person/people, ask Jesus to give you what you need to stay strong and turn away.
- Apologize to the Lord for being impatient or disobedient where you know you should have made better choices. Choose to trust and obey.
- If God is putting it on your heart that you have wounds from past relationships, start to deal with them. Ask Him to help you forgive, bless, and pray for them. Release regrets and pain to Him.

Dear Lord,

Please protect me from the enemies plans to bring back any Ex's from the past. I know the enemy often tries to bring them into our lives to harm us, please help with that. If I still have any attachments or feelings for the people I've been with in the past, please destroy them. If I ever run into an ex of mine, give me strength to walk away. Please forgive me if I have made poor choices or disobeyed You when I knew I shouldn't communicate with certain people.

I forgive each of my ex's now and ask that You please bless and help them. I release any pain, regrets, and wounds from all my relationships to You. If I don't feel I can forgive and let go, help me get to a place where I can. Please continue to teach and help me forgive any ex's, or people, who have hurt me.

In Jesus name, amen.

Dealing with Breakdowns

There are times when we are attacked by the enemy through our minds which then effects our emotions. Crying and releasing our feelings in a healthy way is good, getting angry and throwing a fit is not. Especially if you take it out on the Lord.

Once, I was crying and having what I call a "breakdown". I was frustrated that I was still single in my late twenties and tired of waiting. Jesus kindly brought something I had read to my mind;

> "Satan usually deceives people into thinking that the source of their misery or trouble is something other than what it really is. He wants them to think they are unhappy due to what is going on around them (their circumstances), but the misery is actually due to what is going on inside them (their thoughts)."[1]

Jesus was reminding me that I was not feeling unhappy and upset because of being single or the other circumstances in my life. I was unhappy because of what I had been thinking, negative, angry, and doubtful thoughts about God. The enemy often uses "triggers" to send us off down a wrong thinking path. If we except these thoughts, they effect our emotions and eventually our actions.

Each person is made unique and for that reason has different things that upset them. The enemy knows this, and is watching to see if you take the bait. Preparing in advance is a wise idea. Ask Jesus to alert you to upcoming attacks and any areas of weakness the enemy will try to use against you. At first, these thoughts may be hard to spot these thoughts, but with the Lord's help and some practice it will become easier.

Try It:

- List some things that you feel may be triggers for you, whether they are thoughts, emotions, or circumstances.
- Ask Jesus to alert you the next time the enemy tries to use these triggers. Pray for His help and strength in these areas.
- Last, ask Jesus to begin to destroy these weak areas and heal you.

Let Jesus take your place

Sometimes break downs can be triggered by memories, especially painful ones. Late one night, when I couldn't fall asleep, I quietly sang a song to myself. As I said the lyrics, "I love you and, I understand, that You stand where I stand."[2] I thought about the words and about how Jesus died for us. He is more than able to swap places with us. Not only can He stand in our place of pain and take the blow I believe He wants to.

Often when we feel we are having a mental breakdown, it's because something is festering in our souls. Sometimes the Lord allows our pains to be brought to the surface so we can't ignore them anymore. When you find yourself struggling, take a moment to be still and sort through your feelings. Ask Jesus to help you identify any areas of pain He is trying to heal. If you have many painful memories, I encourage you to write them down and go through each one. Hand them over to Jesus and let him trade places with you. If it helps, visualize Jesus standing in your place.

For example, when I was in high school, I had a teacher that was quite strange. He would often, randomly, in the middle of class say to a student, "Watch out! There's a bomb under your desk!" Whenever this happened, we had to respond by leaving the class room for a few moments. One day the bomb landed under my desk. "Hannah! There's a bomb under your desk! Quick get up!" At this time I was extremely shy and in momments like these I would freeze up. When you're nervous, you sometimes do things that don't make sense.

I was too afraid to get up and leave with the whole class watching me. My mind felt foggy. The teacher wasn't backing down though, and eventually I had to get up. Instead of walking out into the hall, I decided to stand in the corner of the class, my back to the room. The teacher looked at me oddly and said, "That's what you'd do if there was a bomb under your desk? Stand in the corner?" He told me to go sit down, which I did, mortified and embarrassed.

This is one of my most awful memories. It made me feel shameful. I decided a while ago to hand it over to Jesus so He can stand in my place. Instead of me standing in that corner, it's Him. The pain of that memory has been lifted, but at times I still need to remind myself to let go and let Jesus stand there. He can do the same for you, let Him stand where you stand.

Dear Jesus,

I ask that You please come stand in my most humiliating, and painful memories. When these memories are popping up and causing me to mistrust or doubt You, please help me. At times the enemy tries to attack my mind. Sometimes I fail and give in, believing lies. Please forgive me for doing that and help me be ready for any future attacks. Destroy any triggers the enemy uses to get me upset.

Remind me that it's not my circumstances that make me unhappy but negative toxic thoughts I choose to believe. I command every one of these thoughts to leave right now in the name of Jesus Christ. Forgive me for being upset with You when I should be trusting. Help me grow stronger so I can defeat the enemy and his plans. Help me go through memories and experiences and let You take my place.

Amen

Feeling Desperate

If impatience is left to grow, it can quickly turn into desperation. To better understand desperation, it helps to take a look at the definition:

- "Feeling, showing, or involving a hopeless sense that a situation is so bad as to be impossible to deal with"
- "Having lost hope"
- "Giving no ground for hope"
- "Moved by despair or utter loss of hope"
- "Involving or employing extreme measures in attempt to escape defeat or frustration" [1]

There's a theme here that's easy to spot; loss of hope. This is also another way of saying we feel weak and our strength has dried up. It's hard to hope when our circumstance doesn't appear hopeful, or when we don't feel it. That's why you'll often have to choose to hope in God.

Isaiah 40:31 says, "Those who hope in the Lord will
   renew their strength "(NIV).

The word used for "hope" in Hebrew here also means "to wait for, tarry for, look for".[2] When feeling desperate often we're tempted to try and move on without God. Instead of waiting for the person God has planned for us to be with, out of desperation we date people he doesn't approve of. We respond to a text or phone call we know should be ignored. Choosing to trust and wait for the Lord is the opposite of rebelling. It requires us to humble ourselves and submit to God's plan, even when we feel like giving in to our own desires.

By doing this Isaiah says we will not only gain renewed strength, but also;

"They shall mount up with wings like eagles, They
   shall run and not be weary, They shall walk and not
   faint"(Isaiah 40:31, NKJV).

When we make choices that reflect our hope and trust in the Lord, He will give us the strength to mount up above our circumstances. It is important that we not just say we trust the Lord, but actively show it. While God works on our situations, He gives us new strength to run forward and not faint. Maintaining hope is essential. "Hope is the confident expectation of what God has promised, and its strength is in His faithfulness."[3]

Remember *You are Loved*

In times of desperation, we often choose to do stupid things that end up hurting us. I read a quote that I feel gets to the core of why we do this; "Desperate girls do desperate things when they don't feel loved."[4]

How many times do we react out of desperation instead of trusting that the Lord loves us and will work everything out? I'm sure this hurts Him as much as it hurts us. If you feel tempted to do something desperate, ask your self if you have forgotten how much God loves you. When we feel loved, cherished, and cared about, we react differently to hard situations then when we feel the opposite. While we should not rely on feelings, but rather on knowing, at times feeling God's love is what we need.

Ask the Lord to allow you to feel His presence and love, reminding you that He is with you. Take the time out to pray, fast, and study scriptures about God's love for you. The more you get it on your mind and in your thoughts, the more you will live like it's true. The Lord has a husband picked out for you. However, if you act out in desperation and choose to be with someone the Lord doesn't approve of, you risk never meeting the person God has for you.

Remind yourself that you are loved without conditions or requirements. Reject the temptation to act out in lonely desperation. Those actions will only harm you in the long run, and the longings they fill are temporary.

FIGHTING desperation with submission

One way to fight against rebellion and the temptation to make desperate choices is with submission. We are called to resist the devil and his temptations, and instead submit ourselves to the Lord.

> "Submit yourselves then to God, resist the devil, and
> he will flee from you" (James 4:7 NIV).

The word "Submit" used in this verse means to "place under rank to, under God's arrangement, i.e. submitting to the Lord (His plan)." [5]

In order to resist the devil and acting on our own feelings, we must first acknowledge we are below God in rank, meaning we are under Him. His plans for us are better then anything we can dream up, and it would be plain stupid to react by choosing to follow our own desires above His.

I know that sometimes the enemy feels stronger than us, but remember that through Jesus, we have authority over the Devil.

> "Then the seventy returned with joy, saying, "Lord, even the demons are subject to us in Your name"(Luke 10 :17, NKJV).

The word "subject" in the Greek text is the same word used above in James 4:7. The disciples were excited because they realized that in Jesus' name they had authority over the devil. The enemy was "subject" in rank to them, that means he had to obey the disciples. This fight can become easier when you acknowledge that you're under Jesus's authority, and that He's given you the ability to cast out your enemy.

WHEN YOU'RE FEELING DESPERATE, pray for contentment.

A few years back, I got an email from my Grandma. I opened it and read the short phrase, which were written in French;

> "Je tu aime, je tu adore, que veux tu de mois encore?"
> (I love you, I adore you, what more do you want of me?)

While my Grandma probably sent me this because she

knew I was taking French classes, as soon as I read it I felt God was speaking to me.

During that time in my life I was feeling frustrated and dissatisfied. I wanted to go on dates and have a boyfriend, to meet new people, and move forward. I didn't realize it, but I was being ungrateful. I was living like God wasn't enough, like He wasn't doing enough for me. Those words struck my heart. I felt like God was saying, "I adore you so much, I have given you everything, even my Son to save you. What more could you possibly want?" The truth is I was taking God for granted.

When you're feeling discontent, or you feel something is not right in your spirit, stop and ask yourself if you have begun to take God for granted. Our desires, no matter how strong, should never allow us to be pushed so far that we fail to appreciate all that the Lord has done for us. If you feel like this is something you may have done, apologize and ask God to forgive you. Remind yourself how much He's done for you, and thank Him.

Dear Lord,

At times I feel desperation well up in me, and I want to go my own way. As the years pass, I grow impatient, and it often feels more difficult to hope and trust You. Please forgive me for the times I've fallen short in these areas. Help me hope in You so I can mount up above the problems and attacks the enemy tries to throw at me. Help me to renew my strength in You.

When I forget how much You love me, and start to give in to thoughts of desperation, please remind me. If I do not fully understand the depth of Your unconditional love for me, or even what true love is, please teach and show me. Help me be humble and submissive to what Your plan is for my life, and give me strength when this feels impossible to do. When I am tempted to get mad or frustrated with You, remind me how much You love me. Also remind me how much smarter and wiser You are than me.

Please forgive me for every time I have taken You for granted. I know You have my best interest in mind. Please give me more contentment, especially when I'm feeling desperate.

In Jesus name, amen

The Question

We ask it openly at times, and during others we wonder it silently to ourselves. It's more of a fear than a question, "What if God wants me to be single forever, and I never get married?" This is a common lie the enemy uses to push us towards taking matters into our own hands. If left unresolved between you and God, this fear will grow and cause trouble.

Thankfully, there are some encouraging words from Jesus that will help clear things up. It starts with Jesus discussing marriage and divorce with the pharisees in Matthew chapter nineteen (It would be a good idea to read the whole section to get the full context). At the end of the discussion, Jesus says,

> "I tell you that anyone who divorces his wife, except for sexual immorality, and marries another woman commits adultery"(Matthew 19:9, NIV).

In reply, the Disciples say;

> "If this is the situation between a husband and wife, it is better not to marry"(Matthew 19:10 NIV).

Jesus then makes this eye opening statement;

> "Not everyone can *accept* this word, but *only those to whom it has been given"* (Matthew 19:11 NIV, Emphasis mine).

The word "accept" here, in Greek, actually means "to make room or space; (figuratively) to live with an *open* heart."[1] Understand what Jesus is saying here. Not all people will be willing to make room for the concept of being celibate in their hearts, *unless* it has been given to that person by the Lord.

If you are afraid that the Lord wants you to live your life in celibacy, don't be. Jesus is saying here that not everyone is willing to open their hearts to God's will of celibacy, only those who have that gift placed upon them. If you have strong desires to get married, to share your life with a husband, have kids and so on, chances are high that God has marriage planned for you. However, if you feel in your heart you have the gift of celibacy, it's a very special gift not many are given. Jesus continues on;

> "For there are eunuchs who were born that way, and there are eunuchs who have been made eunuchs by others—and there are those who choose to live like eunuchs for the sake of the kingdom of heaven. The one who *can* accept this should accept it" (Matthew 19:12 NIV, Emphasis mine).

The Greek word for Eunuch can mean "alone in bed" (i.e. without a marriage partner).[2] He says that some people are born with no other choice but to be celibate, while others have that choice taken from them. Last, some choose that life for the sake of God's business, much like apostle Paul.

The word used at the end of verse twelve, "can", actually means, "to show *ability* (power); *able* (*enabled* by God), *empowered*" in the Greek text.[3] In other words, those who have the ability and power from God are the ones who make room in their hearts to receive the gift of celibacy and live it out.

While there may be exceptions, I don't believe God would give you strong desires for marriage and intimacy if you were meant to be celibate. Choose to stop giving into that fear and realize the Godly desires you have are there because He made you that way.

TRY IT:

- The gift of singleness and the gift of celibacy (lifelong singleness) are different. If you are single, you have the gift of singleness! Are you using your gift for Jesus?
- Give your fear of being single forever to the Lord, and choose to trust His plans for your life.

Dear Jesus,

The enemy often tries to get me, and others, with a fear of being alone and single forever. Especially during this season, it's one of his favorite lies to use. Please help me overcome this lie. Help me see the truth behind Your words in Matthew and trust that if I were meant to be celibate, I would feel differently about marriage. (If I am made to be celibate, help me joyfully make room for this gift.) Help me trust You and get rid of this fear. I willingly hand it over to You now. Please teach, and help me, use my gift of being single for You. Even if it is hard at times.

Waiting For The Right Time

Awakening love before God's appointed time often creates painful longings in us that cannot be fulfilled. For example, let's say you're watching a romantic movie and you're taking in images of romance and love. It shouldn't come as a surprise if in the following days you find yourself daydreaming about your future spouse and in turn start to wish you weren't single. Watching these types of films and reading romantic books can awaken feelings of love in us before the time is right. The Shulumite, the women speaker in *Song of Solomon,* gives this advice to women;

> "I charge you, O daughters of Jerusalem, By the gazelles or by the does of the field, Do not stir up nor awaken love Until it pleases" (Song of Solomon 2:7, NKJV).

It's repeated several times throughout the book so the reader understands what she's saying is important. When you decide to awaken love, instead of letting God, it will make this season of singleness harder. Choose to turn off the tv, put down the book, and turn away.

THE BEAUTIFUL THING about waiting for God to awaken love is that the process is protected and special. It's much like a closed rose. As a rose is forming and growing, it stays tightly shut. This protects it while it matures from things like insects, fungus, and anything that would like to harm it. If someone where to try and force the little bud open before it was time, it would end up wilted and possibly dead.

Like the rose bud, the Lord makes sure to keep His daughter's love protected and sealed. When we choose to live as God's children, He hides us from the enemy, and any intruders who would harm us. Stirring love is a fragile process that takes time and care. When a rose begins to bloom, each petal unfolds until the rose is fully open. This also means the rose is now exposed, and vulnerable. After the Lord has unfolded each petal, He will make sure you're mature and prepared to fight any intruders off.

Because this process is so fragile and sacred, always choose to let God do the awakening. You can be assured that He knows what He's doing and that He'll protect you. As you are stirred up and prepared for love, there may be "insects" that try to worm their way in, as well as swarm around you. When we are awakened to love, we may attract people who we have no business being around. During this time keep careful guard and watch over your heart and mind. Pray about the guys you choose to be around, even if they are just friends, and ask God for wisdom.

My Grandma sent an email once that I think illustrates this process well;

"The flower does not come to the bee, it blossoms and then the bee comes. Hope your bloom attracts the bee." -J.P.

Dear Father,

May You please continue to protect me as You open up my heart and prepare me for my future relationship. If the enemy tires to send guys to hurt or manipulate me, please plainly show me that and help me turn away. Make me strong so I can fight off any intruders sent to harm me. Give me wisdom in discerning which guy You have planned for me. Help me be patient during this process and allow You to do the unfolding instead of me.

In Jesus Name Amen

While You're Waiting

During the times when you find yourself waiting for the next season, be cautious not to "eat the bread of idleness". As the months or years pass on, it can be easy to fall into a routine. Our mindset may grow dull, as the excitement and passion we once had for the Lord starts to vanish. It can be tempting to direct your passions at something that is not God's purpose for you, or that will lead you down an idle path. To avoid this, we need to look to Jesus' example.

If you read through the stories of Jesus' life, it's clear that He was never idle or lazy, but always working. There where times He was so tired from working that He slept through a storm. Other moments He was grieved to the point of death, yet still took the time to pray for His disciples and everyone who would come to know Him. Through each trial He faced, He always choose to do something, whether it was pray, use His faith, or cast out the enemy. He never chose to be idle. No matter how hard your season of singleness feels, take Jesus's example and choose to do something.

Two definitions of idle are;

- "avoiding work, lazy"
- "without purpose or effect; pointless."[1]

That's exactly what your season of singleness will become if you choose to be idle, it will lack purpose. Think about the term when used to describe an engine running idle, "to run at low power and often disconnected usually so that power is not used for useful work."[2] When we choose to be idle and lazy, the Lord's power is not being used for useful work. Proverbs 31:27 says;

"She watches over the affairs of her household and
　　does not eat the bread of idleness" (NIV).

This is a great verse to study now because not only will it help you while you are single, but also help you prepare to be a Godly wife. The word "watches" in the Hebrew means "to look about, keep watch, spy"[3]. The Godly women described in this verse keeps very careful watch over her household and is perceptive to the way it runs and the flow of it, which requires wisdom. When the enemy tried to offer her a piece of sluggishness she refused to eat it.

While you are single you can start practicing these habits. While you may not have the same type of household as a married women, you can watch over the affairs of your body, which is God's temple. You can watch over the affairs of your apartment or house you share with roommates or parents. The Bible specifically tells us to keep watch because the enemy is constantly looking for a place to strike. Do your best to "spy" out the ways of the type of household God has given you, taking good care of it and taking action to protect it. When you start to feel like it's pointless or like being lazy in your pursuit, refuse to eat the bread of idleness. Developing this habit now will prepare you to be a Godly wife who knows how to keep watch and run the household God will give you in the future.

Dear Jesus,

Help me be like You in my time being single. You were always working no matter how hard things got. I admit sometimes I get tired or overwhelmed by things in life, like the evil in the world or sadness at loosing someone. During these times the enemy pressures me to give up or fill those areas with something idle. Other times I just feel lazy and crabby. Please may You help me to press on during each season and trial. Give me Your strength to not eat the bread of idleness. Teach and help me watch over my household and ways of life that You have given me.

Amen

Preparing For The Future

Preparing for marriage is something you should start doing now. Not only is the enemy destroying marriages, but as Christians, we are supposed to set an example for the people around us. If our marriages and relationships are no different then the world's, what does that say about us? We are meant to be ambassadors for Christ, and it's destructive when we act in ways that go against the Lord's desires. It would be wise to start preparing your heart and mind by weeding out things that need to go. Ask the Lord to help you in praying about specific areas and what to prepare for. He will guide you towards the first step, and help you continue on.

One of the most important steps in this process is realizing you are in a covenant relationship with the Lord, much like a marriage. Marriage is designed to be a reflection of Christ and the church, but also our relationship with Him. First work on your relationship with God, then everything you need to do before marriage will fall into place. The more intimate your relationship with the Lord is, the more prepared you will be for marriage.

PREPARING FOR THE FUTURE

In a marriage you are expected by God to remain faithful to your spouse, even when you don't feel like it. It's the same in your relationship with the Lord. You are expected to remain faithful to Him even when you don't feel like it. I can remember a while back I was sitting on the steps leading to my bedroom thinking about my relationship with God. At the time I was a new Christian, and I understood little. As I pondered the Lord's love for us I felt, spiritually, a wedding band on my ring finger.

It is startling how much God really loves us, to the extent that He views us in a covenant relationship. That means He wants to protect You, comfort You, and be deeply close with you. He wants You to share Your deepest hurts as well as joys with Him. This also means that when we are unfaithful to the Lord, by lusting for things to take His place, engaging in sin, or even making relationships an idol, He views it much the same as a married person would view their spouse cheating on them. Be aware of your shortcomings and how you are treating the Lord.

TRY IT:

- Try studying more on God's love for you, and how serious He views your relationship: Isaiah 54:5, Ezekiel 16:8, Hosea 2:19-20,
- Jesus desires a close, intimate relationship with you. Consider how much time you spend fantasizing and pouring your feelings, emotions, and time into a boyfriend or even the prospect of having one. Realize that Jesus desires you to redirect that towards Him in a Godly way.
- Fasting is a great way to strengthen the connection between you and God. It's also great for gaining

clarity in life, understanding the Bible, and jumpstarting a stale phase in your relationship with the Lord. Consider doing the type of fast God puts on your heart.

ASKING For Advice

I recommend starting to prepare for marriage by asking Godly couples their advice. Specifically, ask them what to pray for while you are single. Below are a few experiences and comments I have received from married people I hope you'll find helpful.

My friend was hosting a movie night a few years back, and I had asked God for a chance to talk to her about marriage and what to pray for. We ended up being too busy to chat, and instead I found myself talking to Regina. As I was curled up on my friends couch she was rocking in a hefty arm chair. Regina was young, married, and pregnant. I felt God was answering my prayer, but in a different way than I expected. So, as she lovingly placed her hand on her growing stomach, I asked her how I should prepare for my future marriage.

She admitted it was hard staying pure, and she and her husband had made a few mistakes intimately before they married. While they remained virgins until their wedding night, she regretted giving into temptations. She suggested praying now for strength to stay pure until married. Plan to set boundaries when you do meet that person, as well as limiting time alone that could lead to intimate situations.

Regina added that it's important to be the first to apologize, in a humble way. This is something we should practice now in all of our relationships. Apologizing includes asking for forgiveness. In some circumstances it also means forgiving. There may be times when you and your future husband say hurtful things to each other, and developing these habits now will prepare you for then. When this feels difficult, remind yourself;

> "Therefore, as *the* elect of God, holy and beloved, put on tender mercies, kindness, humility, meekness, long suffering; bearing with one another, and forgiving one another, if anyone has a complaint against another; even as Christ forgave you, so you also *must do"* (Colossians 3: 12-13, NKJV).

I DID GET a chance to chat with my other friend, Vanessa, at a different time. The first piece of advice she gave was, "Marriage is not for the selfish."

The definition of selfish is;

> "Concerned excessively or exclusively with oneself : seeking or concentrating on one's own advantage, pleasure, or well-being without regard for others."[1]

Jesus let me know once that it is very hard to be married if you are a selfish person. According to 1 Corinthians 13:5, a characteristic of love is that it "does not seek its own". In other words, love is not selfish and self centered. If you are living a selfish life, you are not living in love. If you don't develop God's love now, how will you live it out in your future marriage? It would be wise to study the entire list of love's characteristics listed in the two verses of 1 Corinthians, ask the Lord to help you develop this type of love.

My friend also told me to pray against backsliding while married. I feel this relates back to remaining faithful in your relationship with God. Everyone makes mistakes. Ecclesiastes 7:20 says;

> "Indeed, there is no one on earth who is righteous, no one who does what is right and never sins" (NIV).

However, backsliding is choosing to sin and continuing to make that choice when you know it's wrong. This is something most Christians struggle with at times. If you need to, admit to God your shortcomings and desire to sin, and ask for His help. It's better to learn how to humble our selves in this way now then when are married and struggling.

Last, Venessa went on to say there was times in her marriage when her and her husband where not growing in the Lord. They were experiencing a spiritual lapse, or in other words, a failure of concentration on what was actually important, Jesus. She said that Christ being the family's center and leader is important if we desire to avoid spiritual droughts as well as a healthy, joyful marriage.

Dear Lord,

May You please forgive me for all the times I have not remained faithful to You. Help me to start doing that and live it out as I grow in You. Please also help me develop a close and intimate relationship with You. Especially during this time of being single. There are moments when I wish I had a person to spend special time with. Help me through these times and to learn to spend them with You.

In Proverbs 12:15 it says, "The way of fools seems right to them, but the wise listen to advice" (NIV). Help me be wise Lord, and listen to advice instead of always going off of what I think is right. Please put good, Godly people around me and in my life that I can seek advice from, especially in marriage. Help me see outside of myself, noticing others. Teach and help me get rid of selfishness and self centeredness.

In Jesus Name, Amen

Breaking Barriers

A few years back, I hopped into bed, got comfortable, when suddenly I had a realization come to me. It was so random and clear, I knew it was from God;

"To live shame free is to live without barriers".

Then I felt Jesus urging me to write it down, so I typed it out in the notes section of my phone. At the time, I knew it meant something important, but I didn't fully understand what.

Shame is more than guilt, it's a feeling that something is deeply wrong with who you are. Here's a good definition;

"As a self-conscious emotion, shame informs us of an internal state of inadequacy, unworthiness, dishonor, regret, or disconnection."[1]

One of the main things shame can create, even without us knowing it, is disconnection and barriers. It creates a wall between us and the Lord when we hide or keep stuff from

Him. It's the same with people. These barriers can also hinder making meaningful connections with people and deepening our relationship with Jesus. If you find yourself having a hard time doing either, both, or feel that something is blocking you from experiencing the Lord's love, shame may be part of the problem.

Dealing with this now, while single, is necessary to having a healthy future marriage and family. Shame hurts a married couples ability to be one with each other. As the author of *Sacred Sex* puts it; "Shame erects a barrier to enjoying Godly intimacy...". He also mentions that shame and self condemnation can create a brick wall that separates us from our loved ones.[2]

SHAME LIKES TO HIDE.

Shame is one of those things that likes to stay hidden. It's sneaky, getting in without us knowing it, and staying like an unwanted guest hiding in the basement. In order to find it, we need to go down the stairs and flip on the lights, searching every hidden spot. In order to heal we need to learn how to stand before the Lord unashamed. We need to understand we are unconditionally accepted and loved by the Lord the way we are, flaws and all.

Studying and memorizing Romans 8:38 is a great way to start clearing out shame;

> "For I am convinced that neither death nor life,
> neither angels nor demons, neither the present nor
> the future, nor any powers, neither height nor
> depth, nor anything else in all creation, will be able
> to separate us from the love of God that is in
> Christ Jesus our Lord" (Romans 8:38-9, NIV).

Paul is saying in this verse he's confident nothing has the power or is even capable of separating us from the Lord's love. That word "separate" in the Greek text can also mean "divide". [3] You can find comfort in the fact that you are loved no matter what, and nothing can divide you from Jesus's love, even shame. The Lord will never stop loving you, and does so without conditions. One definition of unconditional is;

"With no limits in any way : without restriction by conditions or qualifications."[4]

He loves us without any limits. Unlike us, Jesus does not need to get to know you in order to develop a deep love for you. He already knows you completely and loves you.

There are no standards you have to meet for God to love you, nor does your past make you unworthy of His love. If you are afraid to stand before God and be open with Him, remember that He loves you no matter what. Nothing you admit, say or do will change that.

Maybe you are like me, a perfectionist. You're afraid to be open with Jesus, and that He may change the way He sees you if you are. That is a lie, and if you search your heart Jesus will show you the truth. No matter how dirty your past feels or was, He still feels the same about you. While He detests our sins, He still loves us.

Take Paul for example, he helped murder the Lord's chosen people, His children. Paul persecuted Jesus's church, and being His body, Paul was persecuting Jesus Himself. Jesus still loved Paul, and saw what he could and would be. In Acts 9:15, Jesus said that Paul was His chosen instrument that He would use to reach people. Even after all Paul had done, Jesus deliberately chose him.

You are also Jesus's chosen instrument. The devil will try to tell you that your past dictates your life and future, and that the Lord can't use you. For many of us, our mistakes and the mistakes of others have created wounds and shame. Your past may have molded who you are, but it does not ultimately make you who you are unless you let it.

According to the Bible you are now an unconditionally loved daughter. Jesus does not desire for you to feel ashamed, He desires to use you. Shame is a lie that the enemy has fabricated. Unconditional acceptance and love is part of curing shame, along with exposing the places and memories it hides in. We need to learn to accept unconditional love from the Lord so we can better give Godly love to our future spouse and family.

SHAME EFFECTS the way we see ourselves, often negatively. It tries to make us feel second class, used, and of little worth. The Lord teaches us that we are worth more than we can comprehend. We are precious and highly valued treasures in the Father's eyes. When you realize you are His daughter and He loves you unconditionally, without any standards to meet, it will change your relationship with Him. It will drive out fear. Instead of doing things because you're afraid of disappointing Him, or because you should, you'll do it simply because you love Him. Your intimacy will grow deeper, and you'll feel free to express your love to God in your own creative ways. Most importantly you won't feel uncomfortable around the Lord.

Shame tells us we can't feel relaxed and comfortable in the Lord's presence because we have something we need to hide. We may feel that if He sees who we really are, He won't accept us. You will always be unconditionally loved and accepted. Practice thinking about the truth of this fact, even if it feels hard to grasp. When we feel truly comfortable with the Lord, barriers the enemy has created will be removed. Having no negative barriers is a powerful thing.

Dear Lord,

I some times struggle with feeling ashamed of myself around others and around You. Things in my past have created painful memories. At times, I see myself as something worthless and unusable. Forgive me and continue to reveal to me that this is a lie. Show me the truth about who I am in You and teach me to see myself in that way.

Please dig up and help me deal with any memories or things that shame is using to hide in. Shine Your love on each area. Teach me and help me understand Your unconditional love and what it means to be a daughter, specifically Your daughter. Please give me a knowing that nothing can ever separate me from Your love and acceptance. Continue to break down each barrier shame creates so I can live freely in You and with others.

I ask this in Jesus name, amen.

How You Think About Singleness

You may have heard the saying, "Change your thoughts, change your life." There's truth in it, and it applies to what we think while single. At times a big part of why being single hurts is because of our negative attitudes, thoughts, and feelings. Jesus has called us to renew our minds and think on things that are only good, noble and praiseworthy. Being negative and wallowing in self pity won't add anything good to your life, and it certainly won't make you feel better.

In the American culture we often view singleness and solitude as a something negative. While God has made us to live in communities and families, there are seasons when we need to step away from that and spend time in solitude with God. Jesus did this often;

> "But Jesus often withdrew to the wilderness for prayer" (Luke 5:16, NLT).

Other versions use the phrase "lonely places" to describe the place Jesus went to. The point is that He purposely withdrew to spend time praying and preparing away from people. As one article puts it so well;

"Jesus' solitude is how he went deeper in his love-relationship with the God he knew as Abba. Jesus invites us to join him." [1]

Being single means we have more of this special alone time to spend with the Lord. We should choose to use and see it as something positive like Jesus who, as we know, was also single.

In the world of Hollywood, being single is usually illustrated as something negative. I can't remember the last time I saw a movie or show where singleness was portrayed as it actually is; a time of opportunity. Yes, it can be lonely, and no it's usually not easy, but we are seeing it through a negative lens. The reality depicted in movies is a lie, and the majority of it lacks Biblical truth. Be aware of your feelings towards singleness and regularly evaluate them, making sure they line up with truth.

There's a quote from the book "Battlefield of The Mind" that I like to read when I'm starting to get negative,

> "Positive thoughts are full of faith and hope. Negative thoughts are full of fear and doubt."[2]

Choose to start being positive, focus on creating thoughts filled with faith. We are Christ's ambassadors, so always remember you are setting an example.

Along with negative thoughts, be aware of negative feelings. While feelings usually start with thoughts, at times they can linger even after we've changed our thinking. That's when we need to cast out these feelings, and prepare to guard yourself by thinking obedient thoughts and resisting the devil. Guard your mind with Bible verses and meditate on God's goodness and character. When the enemy comes around with his lies, you'll be ready. You won't bite into the lie that God has favorites, that he's forgotten about you, or that he doesn't care.

Singleness can be a great opportunity for growth. Spend time developing your character in the Lord and maturing. Figure out your weak points and ask God to make them strong and usable. Get to know people on a deeper level, and most importantly, help them. Do something for the Lord during this time, and enjoy it, it won't come around again. If you are aware of what God wants you to do, and His plans for your life, start doing them now. Not many people openly and positively embrace their time being single, and when they do it's inspiring to others.

WHEN IT DOES GET TOUGH, here are some phrases to say or think on that will help you stay positive and motivated;

- "My grace is sufficient for you, for My power is made perfect in weakness"(2 Corinthians 12:9).
- Being single can be hard at times, but I know I am not alone, the Father is with me. Jesus always does life with me whether I sense it or not.
- Because of my singleness in this season, I now have more time to commit to the Lord and loving others. I can spend this time to heal, learn, and prepare for the future.
- There is no reason to be discouraged. The Lord has me engraved on the palm of His hand, He will never leave me, and hasn't forgotten about me or my prayers.

- Today may be rough, but the Lord can use this to develop compassion in me for others who are experiencing the same thing. In the long run, my pain will be transformed into fruit.

Side Notes on PMS: *Do's and Don'ts*

For some girls, our monthly cycle can be a challenge, emotionally and mentally. Our body goes through hormonal changes that make life feel high some days and low on others. On these low days, we sometimes crave attention or affection to comfort us. The enemy especially likes to attack our emotions and thoughts during this time. I can't speak for every experience, since we're all different, but here is a list that discusses some issues you may face.

Do:

- Spend extra time with God. Some girls are more sensitive during their monthly cycle or leading up to it. Use this as an advantage. Being sensitive means you can pick up on things you may otherwise miss. Read the Bible more, and allow God to show you new things. Pray more, and listen to what the Lord says to you. Have a quiet time of worship with the Lord. If you notice someone around you seems to be hurting, help them.
- Allow the Lord to comfort you. Be open with Him about your emotions and feelings, and consider writing them out. Ask for His strength and help in each area. Remember that He understands, after

all He did create your body to have a monthly cycle.
- Ask the Holy Spirit to reveal to you any areas where you are believing lies concerning your period. For example, we are often told that women are more emotional and moody during this time. While this may happen now and then, it doesn't make it true for every period, or for every girl. "For as he thinks in his heart, so he is" (Proverbs 23:7 NKJV). Think good thoughts about yourself and your emotions.
- Ask Jesus for grace to handle your emotions and the uncomfortable times of having a period. Pray for wisdom in discerning any attempts of the enemy to take advantage of you during this time. Be on the look out for the enemy trying to manipulate your emotions or feelings. Ask God to protect you.
- Exercise regularly, especially cardio. Aerobic exercises (and others) can help keep you regular, and it boosts your endorphins. While cardio during our period is not always an option, I've found just doing it regularly throughout the month will help.
- Start choosing to eat healthy. Our bodies are the Lord's temple, and we should treat them as such. Eating healthy is important for our overall well being and some say it helps with PMS symptoms. While I feel it's okay to have a small amount of the junk food while craving, it's better to go for something healthy.
- Ask for quality time with someone you love. Watch or do something that makes you laugh, and take time to relax. Especially be careful of your

thoughts. The enemy likes to attack us while we are going through things, and periods can be a good opportunity. Watch out for negative thoughts of depression, irritation, or anger. Practice disciplining your emotions, releasing any tendencies to overreact to the Lord.

Don't

- Don't give into negative or self degrading thoughts.
- Don't lash out or over react.
- Don't overwork or exhaust yourself.
- Don't make it an excuse for being lazy, skipping spending time with the Lord, or making unhealthy choices.
- Don't complain or whine about things that are bothering you, instead think of some things you are thankful for.
- Don't try to fill your emotional needs with things that aren't God or related to Him, such as excessive shopping, romance movies, food ect.
- Don't watch, read, or listen to any romantic things that you know may stir up your emotions and make you feel a strong desire for a boyfriend/husband.
- Don't give into temptation or compromise because you aren't feeling your best.

Dear Jesus,

May You please help me view my time being single as a blessing. Help me turn from my negative thoughts about this season. Just like You used Your time being single to do God's will and spend special alone time together, help me do the same. Teach me to see solitude as something positive and that You will use. In any areas that I am viewing singleness in negative ways, forgive me, and help me change my thinking.

I know periods are not always pleasant to deal with. Please have compassion on me and give me Your grace to deal with each one. Help me develop self control and refrain from lashing out or hurting others. If there are things I can change in order to help this time, such as healthier eating habits, please help me do that. Last, help me treat my future husband and family in a Godly way, even when I don't feel like.

Amen.

He Hasn't Forgotten You

"Can a woman forget her nursing child, and not have compassion on the son of her womb? Surely they may forget, yet I will not forget you. See, I have inscribed you on the palms *of My hands;* your walls *are* continually before Me" (Isaiah 49:15-16, NKJV).

There are moments when it feels like God has forgotten us, especially when everyone seems to be receiving what we've been praying for. It's tempting to be jealous, to get frustrated with ourselves and God, but we must stop and remember His promises and power. If He can create the universe He can find and bring you the right husband. Not only is it impossible for God to forget us, it hurts Him when we think He's that kind of Father.

Have you ever written something on your hand so you wouldn't forget it, or so that you could look at it throughout the day? This is the type of metaphor God's using in the verse above. The Hebrew word used for "inscribe" also means "cut into", like the way you would etch an image on a stone.[1] I like how deep that metaphor is, that the Lord loves us so much He etches our image into the palm of His hand so that it can't be removed.

Trust His Timing

A few years back, my boss handed me a present while we were driving. It was a gift for my twenty-third birthday. I peeled the paper off quickly, and stared at the box. My boss looked at me from the drivers seat and jokingly said, "It's a coffee cup, but I just liked the box." It was pretty, with flowers on it, and in the center a Bible verse from Ecclesiastes 3:11, "He has made everything beautiful in His time." I read it, then pulled the cup out, which was equally pretty with the same bible verse on each side. I remember looking at the cup and feeling annoyed though, not at my boss, but at God. I had a sinking feeling that *His* timing meant I would be waiting a while for the things I was praying for.

During that time I had recently re-dedicated my life to the Lord, and as a result, lost most of my friends. I was lonely, mad, and impatient. I didn't want to wait for God's timing, I wanted to make new friends and get married. It felt like He had forgotten to consider how much being lonely can hurt.

It's been almost four years since then, and I'm still waiting for the answers to some of those prayers. I'm not usually patient even now, but what I have learned is that the Lord is aware of our feelings and desires. He doesn't forget our prayers, even after many years pass and time seems to drag on. During these seasons of waiting, He is still actively working. The original verse is phrased like this;

"He has made everything beautiful in its time"
(Ecclesiastes 3:11, NKJV).

Remember the Shulumite women's advice in Song of Solomon, "Do not awaken or arouse love until it pleases" (Song 8:4). I think it pairs nicely with this verse. We have to trust that God's timing is best for love, marriage, and everything else. Though we sometimes wish to be married or have a family, it may not be the right time. This, at least for me, can be hard to accept some days, but understand this doesn't mean God isn't answering your prayers or guiding your future. As we choose to remain faithful to Him, He continues to always work, even when things seem to be moving slow. He is working everything out in His time.

Dealing with Jealousy

> "A sound heart is life to the body, but envy is
>   rottenness to the bones" (Proverbs 14:30, NKJV).

Recognize that the enemy will try to "rot your bones" with jealousy. If you have been thinking and entertaining thoughts of envy, it shouldn't be surprising if you feel tired, crabby, and agitated. The enemy knows if he can get you to envy, and do it consistently, it will grow and fester until you are spiritually sick. Proverbs says that a sound, healthy heart is life to the body. Ask God to help you develop healthy heart, free of envy.

Galatians 5:19 says that Jealousy is a work of the flesh;

> Now the works of the flesh are evident, which are:
>   adultery, fornication, uncleanness, lewdness,
>   idolatry, sorcery, hatred, contentions, **jealousies**,
>   outbursts of wrath, selfish ambitions, dissensions,
>   heresies, **envy**, murders, drunkenness, revelries,
>   and the like; of which I tell you beforehand, just as

I also told *you* in time past, that those who practice such things will not inherit the kingdom of God" (Galatians 5:19-21 NIV, Emphasis mine).

The warning at the end of the verse is pretty clear. Don't let your jealousy and envy turn into a practice. If you find yourself struggling with this regarding the relationships of others, ask yourself if you are jealous in other areas also. If envy is present in one area of your life, it may be lurking in others. Ask Jesus to forgive you, and to help you overcome your flesh and destroy this habit. One way you can start doing this is by asking God to help you further develop love, since one of the characteristics of love is, "It does not envy" (1 Corinthians 13:4, NIV).

WATCH YOUR THOUGHTS AND FEELINGS. The truth is, you don't have to be jealous. Jesus cares about you and knows your every desire and need. When we react or give in to jealousy, it's like saying we don't trust Him. Let's say you run into a friend who just met the love of her life and is happily telling you all about. The enemy is waiting of course, and starts bombarding you with thoughts and feelings of doubt, jealousy, and bitterness. If you have a strong trust in the Lord you will easily recognize these thoughts and feelings. You will quickly banish them because you don't need to be afraid that the Lord won't come through for you. If your faith in God is deep and pure, you will not only trust that he has someone equally wonderful planned for you, you'll *know* it. There will be no question or worry in your mind. Jealousy won't phase you. You will also happily rejoice with your friend.

If you feel pain in a situation like this, it means you still have fears about God taking care of your future. You still have mistrust in your soul. Take time out to work with Jesus on this.

Dear Jesus,

I know in my heart it is impossible for You to forget me, but at times it does feel that way. I get tired of waiting and trying to be patient. Please help me to continue to trust You. When I need to be reminded that You hear my prayers and have not forgotten about me, please do so. Help me understand how Your ways are higher than mine. When the enemy is trying to get me to feel impatient and give up on waiting, give me strength. Teach me to see the beauty of how You make everything beautiful in its time.

Please forgive me for being jealous of others, especially where marriage and relationships are concerned. Sometimes it feels frustrating because I don't want to be envious, but these feelings and thoughts come out of no where. Help me catch these and get rid of them before I allow them to affect me. Give me Your strength when it feels painful to see others receiving what I've been praying for. Help me be happy for them instead of jealous.

Forgive me for not trusting You with my future, and for every doubting, negative thought I've entertained. Help and teach me to believe in You so deeply that I know You have a good marriage planned for me. I ask You to please get the fear, doubt, unbelief out of me right now. Develop in me a love that is not jealous. Stop the enemies plans to rot my bones and teach me to have a sound, peaceful heart.

Amen

Why Am I Still Single?

I've asked God this question more times than I'd like to admit. While we need to remain respectful, I think the Lord doesn't mind our questions, and with the right perspective it can actually be a good thing. Jesus has given me some answers to this question that revealed some things I need to work on before I enter marriage.

A few years back, I got on my knees and asked God if I could meet my future husband soon. The answer came quickly and clearly, "You're not ready for that kind of relationship." Of course I felt disappointed, but I wasn't sure what to make of that answer. After I thought about it, I felt like there was so much to work on, it may take years to sort it all out. That answer made me feel deficient in some way, or like I had to attain something in order to measure up. Both are far from the truth.

NOT READY DOESN'T MEAN NOT *good enough*.

A few years after that prayer, my friend and I walked into a local coffee shop together. We were there for a Bible study, and took two seats at a long wooden table. It was currently packed with girls on each side, already talking and laughing loudly.

The topic for that evening was renewing our minds. The leader kept brining up excellent points she discovered in the book we were reading, and I tried to quickly keep up, writing each down. Without warning, the subject turned towards marriage and singleness. The leader talked about how at times being single is difficult because we feel like something's wrong with us when God has us wait. We don't like to hear that we need to be patient or are not ready for a relationship. Then she said something that made me pause and look up;

"Not ready doesn't mean not good enough."

Something clicked in me when I heard the leader say that. I needed to hear those words. I felt God's warmth fill my soul as I released the lie that I was not "good enough" to get married. I had felt that maybe because of my past, all my mistakes and scars, that God was not allowing me to get married or even date. I was believing what the enemy told me, that someday, maybe, I would reach a point were I finally measured up. *Then* God would allow me to move forward.

Truthfully, if the Lord is telling you that you're not ready for marriage or a relationship, it doesn't mean that something is wrong with you. It doesn't mean you should feel guilty about a tough past, and regret the mistakes you've made. You don't need to measure up, or try to please God before he'll let you move on to marriage.

What we often fail to understand is that God is simply looking out for our best interest. Not ready only means that you are not fully prepared for such an intimate season. Rushing into marriage or relationship before we are ready can lead to unnecessary wounds and even future divorce.

Marriage is a wonderful gift, but it's also something we should take seriously.

Try It:

- As we prepared to finish up the meeting and head home, a newly married girl gave us single ladies some advice; "He is faithful, He comes through. I so wish I would have worried less and trusted Him more." If you have fallen short in this area, ask the Lord to forgive you for worrying and not trusting Him. Then pray He'll help you trust Him.
- Have you been believing the lie that you are not good enough to get married? Ask the Lord to forgive you for believing that lie, and choose to believe that in Him, you are more than enough. Then cast that lie out and renounce it in the name of Jesus Christ.

Renewing your mind

I was laying in bed one morning, frustrated, when Jesus politely informed me, "You can't get married until you renew your mind." I sat up, and thought that over. It was true my mind was frequently a dumping ground for the enemy and I was really struggling in that area. I think sometimes we don't realize how powerful our thoughts are, and the importance of renovating what we think.

Growing up I attended church and went to a Christian school. However, I cannot recall, even once, learning about actively renewing my mind in the Lord and His word. I suppose it's not surprising that later on, whenever Jesus would tell me I needed to renew my mind, I didn't think much of it, let alone do it.

What about you, has anyone ever taught you the importance of renewing your mind? What does it even mean anyway? In short, it means to refresh and retrain your mind to think in a way that aligns with God, His truth, and His word. It is leaving your old mind behind, shaped by the world, and molding it into a mind like Christs'. This takes time, effort, and studying of God's word. It is not something that happens automatically when you give your life to Jesus. Sadly, there are many Christians who love God, but still think like the world.

For some this can be challenging, especially if your past has been hard. Sometimes we let negative, destructive thoughts in without knowing it. Even worse, we choose to believe they are true. The results are worth the effort though. Romans 2:12 says;

> "Do not conform to the pattern of this world, but be *transformed* by the renewing of your mind" (Emphasis mine).

The word "transformed" here is the same word used to describe Jesus' transfiguration on the mountain (see Matt 17:1-8, Mark 9:2-8, Luke 9:28-36).[1] This moment was so life changing that Peter is still struck by it, making mention of the experience in his later writings (see 2 Peter 1:16-18). The point is that when we actively choose to discipline, renew, and change our thinking, we are given the opportunity to be transfigured also. We will be able to distinguish what His will is for our life (Romans 12:2). He will use us to help others and fulfill our destiny in Him.

. . .

In relation to marriage, renewing your mind is a step that needs to be taken and worked through for you to have a Godly and successful relationship and family. When I'm struggling, I often get hit with the thought, "What does renewing your mind have to do with getting married? After all, God lets plenty of people who don't have their minds renewed get married." At first, this seems to be a plausible question. God does let people get married with un-renewed minds. What the enemy doesn't want you to know is that once you are married, he will try to destroy your marriage. Often this starts with ungodly and negative thoughts. Without a renewed mind it will be extremely difficult to get through the bumps without losing something to the enemy.

God also wants you to have the best marriage and life you can possibly have, filled with His thoughts and His love. After all, Jesus gave His life for that. People who jump into a marriage without first working on their mind and thoughts, risk having bad things spring up in the future. Unfortunately, I have seen this first hand.

My parents met when they were young, my mom nineteen, and my Dad in his early twenties. My mother always says she knew she was going to be with my dad for a long time after their first conversation. A year later they got married, and as life moved on they both decided to dedicate their lives to the Lord. Though they were sincere, and loved God, they were never taught about things that are essential to being a healthy Christian. One of these was renewing their minds.

As a result, satan stepped in and took every opportunity he saw. My parents lost touch with God and love in general. They let themselves be deceived by lies in their mind they never knew were there. After twenty plus years of marriage, they divorced. A decision that negatively affected their lives and those around them.

We often forget that our actions, good and bad, ripple out from our lives. Sometimes like pebbles dropped in still water, and sometimes like boulders. If you neglect to heal, and get your thought life in order, you risk negatively affecting yourself and those you love. Training yourself to think Godly thoughts has the power to save your future marriage and family, and your walk with the Lord. Most importantly, when you choose to renew your mind, you will be transformed.

> " Finally, brethren, whatever things are true, whatever things *are* noble, whatever things *are* just, whatever things *are* pure, whatever things *are* lovely, whatever things *are* of good report, if *there is* any virtue and if *there is* anything praiseworthy—meditate on these things" (Philippians 4:8, NKJV).

Dear Jesus,

I realize that renewing my mind in You and what You say is very important. Please help me take the first steps towards doing this, or to continue on. Where the enemy has engrained thinking patterns or views that are not Your will, begin to unravel and destroy them.

Even if I don't fully understand how to do this, help me Lord. Some days feel harder than others, on these days please give me Your grace and strength to keep going. Help me not give up. Please keep encouraging me along the way, showing me where I have made progress. Last, teach me to think like You and get rid of thinking that would be harmful to my future marriage and family. Last, if there are specific things in the way of me moving onto marriage, please gently show them to me. Help me work on each.

Amen

Asking Jesus Exciting Questions

❦

The fun thing about being single is that the idea of your future husband is exciting to think about now. Instead of feeling down because God hasn't introduced you two yet, ask Jesus some questions. For example consider asking Him to show you or give you and impression of what your future husband is like.

A few months back, when I was struggling hardcore with being single and believing that God had someone for me, I prayed this prayer. Jesus showed me in a dream that the guy he had planned for me is very kind, he also gave me a sense of his character, gentle and caring. This helped a lot, giving me more faith to wait patiently. It also gave me something to think about when I am struggling, as well as a realization of the type of man that I would like to be with. God knows the type of person that works best with your personality before you do.

Most importantly, knowing this reminded me that the Lord is in control, has everything planned out, and is way ahead of me in terms of figuring out my life. He is good, and has good things planned for you also. When we stop worrying about our future and life, we are free to enjoy our relationship with Jesus. When we worry, it blocks Him. If you have the desire, ask Jesus to show you what you future husband is like if you think it will lead to positive results. The answer may come in different ways, so keep your eyes and ears open.

SPECIFIC PRAYERS

Another fun thing to do while single is asking the Lord to put on your heart specific prayers for your future husband. Everyone has things they struggle with, and we all go through hard times. Pouring yourself out for someone else is a good way to train yourself not to be self-centered. Equally fun is asking Jesus to tell your future husband to pray for you. Not only is this helpful when you are struggling, it's encouraging and builds your faith. You will realize how special it is that God has a good, loving person prepared for you. You will also begin to understand how powerful prayer is.

I remember quite a few years back, I was going through a rough times. My best friend and I were no longer getting along. What was even harder was that the Lord was telling me it was time to let her go because we were on separate paths. I was sitting on my love seat, almost in tears, when I slowly started to feel better. I felt like some of the pain and weight of a lost friend was lifted. I felt peaceful and able to carry on through the day. I was questioning the sudden change of things when I felt the Lord was telling me that my future husband had just been praying for me. I recall thinking, "Wow, that really helped." I felt the Lord then say, "See how much prayer helped you? Remember to pray for other people so you can help them."

The next exciting suggestion, if you feel it's right for you, is asking Jesus to show you how much time you have left of being single. Sometimes, when it feels like the years are dragging on, it can make waiting harder. Worries start creeping up as yet another friend gets married, and you get that sinking feeling in your heart. Instead of questioning God, ask Him to show you how short the time of you being single really is.

I didn't think to ask Jesus this, but thankfully He showed me. I'm twenty-seven and single. I'll be honest in saying that it's hard for me to be patient, though I am learning to enjoy this time. Jesus showed me that I have a short time left in being single, and that getting married is the next season He has prepared. For me, this was what I needed to hear at exactly the right time. It helped me relax, and not worry so much about the future. Most importantly, it helped me realize I need to do more to prepare for marriage.

I highly recommend that you start praying about your future marriage and your husband now, whether you ask Jesus this question or not. Diligently study what God's word has to say about marriage, including Song of Solomon. Read Christian books on marriage and pray about your findings. Ask the Lord to start transforming your life and heart now.

This question may not be right for everyone to ask. I think if Jesus would have shown me five years ago that I have a chunk of singleness left, I wouldn't have taken the news well. Ask Jesus to do what He knows is best for you.

WRITING notes to your future husband.

Last, if you already write notes to your future husband, great, if not consider giving it a try. I recommend it because it builds your faith. Each time you pray for or write a letter to him, you are using your faith by believing that God has a husband prepared for you. You're saying you trust the Lord so much you're willing to write to and pray for someone you haven't even met. Writing is also a great opportunity to get your feelings or even fears out in a healthy way while simultaneously praying for others.

For this section of prayer, I encourage you to write your own based on what you feel is best for you. Be sure to ask Jesus' advice on what He thinks and His timing.

Why A Single Rose Is Beautiful

There's no doubt that a bouquet of roses is beautiful. But when you see a single rose in a vase, or in someone's hand, there's an elegance it possesses that's not in a bouquet. There's something special about a single rose. You really get to admire its beauty undistracted by the other flowers.

God feels the same way about His single daughters. While He loves all of His children equally, there's something special and different about them. Much like the love a father has for his unmarried daughters. They've been given a season of opportunity. While being single has it's difficulties, it also is a wonderful time to grow closer with the Lord. Actually, I would say that this is one of the main purposes of being single. Keep this in mind on your journey.

He will never leave you

I'd like to close with one of my favorite verses, Hebrews 13:5. It's a beautiful promise that I know will help you. While the amplified version of this verse says it well, the AMPC classic edition gets God's point across even more.

In the original Greek text, three negatives proceed the verb "I will not" so when you read the version below, you really get a better grasp on the extent of God's promise.

> "...for He [God] Himself has said, I will not in any way fail you *nor* give you up *nor* leave you without support. [I will] not, [I will] not, [I will] not in any degree leave you helpless *nor* forsake *nor* let [you] down (relax My hold on you)! [Assuredly not!]" Hebrews 13:5 AMPC.

God will never leave us on this journey. He will be there when you feel your singleness is getting old, if you get married, or whether you don't. During all the seasons of life He will be with you. The best part is that the Lord *wants* to be involved in every part of our life. He never wants us to feel or think we are alone in this.

He may speak to you directly or through your favorite Bible verse, or He may use someone close to you. Sometimes we just need to take a moment and realize how involved God is in our lives whether we see it or not. During this beautiful, yet challenging, time of being single remember God is planning and molding you into something wonderful. It is a sacred time, and one you most likely won't get to live through again. Choose make the most of it.

Dear Father,

I am sorry I don't always see being single as something positive, but I would like to change that. May You please help me as we go through this journey together. I am so happy You have promised You'll never leave me and that You want to be a part of my life until I go home. Please use my season of singleness for Your kingdom and glory. Help me see that it's a special time. Teach me to understand stability in You and that You will always be with me throughout my life, even when it's difficult. Thank you for this time of being single that I can use for You!

Epilogue

I hope you have found encouragement and healing in this little book. Being single is not always a cakewalk. Often times it takes discipline and faith to make it through the bumps. Just remember that Jesus is always with you along the way. In the grand scheme of things, your time being single is, for most, very short. Enjoy this season and all the freedom and growth that comes with it. I have been praying for you while writing this, and I'd like to end with another prayer;

Dear Lord,

I know that I have not really handled being single well. I'm happy that has changed though, thank you. I ask that You do the same for each girl who reads this book. Help them not make the same mistakes that I did, and protect them from the enemy and all his schemes. If they are having a hard time being patient and trusting You, please help them.

Teach them to look for a man who is pure of heart and good, someone who loves You. Help them be patient and wait for the wonderful person You have planned for them. In the waiting, please strengthen and grow Your relationship with them. Remind them that You are with them when they are lonely, and that You know what it's like to be single. Give them Your grace and strength.

I ask this in Jesus name, Amen

Afterword

Book Suggestions for further reading:

- *Praying for Your future Husband: Preparing Your Heart For His, b*y Robin Jones Gunn, and Tricia Goyer
- *Sacred Singleness,* by Leslie Ludy
- *Love Defined,* by Kristen Clark, Bethany Baird
- *The Book of Romance: What Solomon says about Sex Love and Intimacy*, by Tommy Nelson
- *Sacred Sex*, by Tim Allen Gardner
- *31 Days of Praying For Your Future Husband: How the power of a praying women can change her future marriage,* by Caitlyn Burns
- *Prayers for Your Future Husband,* by Hannah L.M.
- *Battlefield of the Mind,* and *Power Thoughts,* by Joyce Meyer

Notes

1. Dealing with Loneliness

1. https://biblehub.com/greek/1411.htm
2. https://biblehub.com/greek/1981.htm
3. https://biblehub.com/greek/5055.htm

2. Trust Him

1. "Trust | Definition of Trust in English by Oxford Dictionaries."*Oxford Dictionaries,English*,Oxford Dictionaries, en.oxforddictionaries.com/definition/trust.
2. https://biblehub.com/hebrew/982.htm
3. https://biblehub.com/hebrew/3820.htm

3. Come to the Lord

1. https://biblehub.com/greek/5312.htm
2. https://biblehub.com/greek/2900.htm
3. https://biblehub.com/greek/1977.htm
4. https://biblehub.com/greek/3199.htm

5. Beautiful, Noble, Honorable

1. https://biblehub.com/greek/2570.htm
2. https://biblehub.com/greek/2570.htm

7. Never Settle

1. Paramore. "Miracle." *Roit*, David Bendeth, House of Loud, New Jersey, 2007, track 7.
2. https://biblehub.com/greek/4347.htm

9. Dealing with Breakdowns

1. Meyer, Joyce, and Joyce Meyer. Battlefield of the Mind: Winning the Battle in Your Mind. Faith Words, 2017. p.69
2. Flyleaf. "I'm Sorry." *Flyleaf,* Howard Benson, Octane records, 2005, track 6.

10. Feeling Desperate

1. "Desperate." *Merriam-Webster*, Merriam-Webster, www.merriam-webster.com/dictionary/desperate.
2. https://biblehub.com/hebrew/6960.htm
3. Chapter I: THE CHRISTIAN HOPE. (2010, April 16). Retrieved from https://onlinelibrary.wiley.com/doi/pdf/10.1111/j.1758-6623.1952.tb01593.x
4. Isom, Mo. Sex, Jesus, and the Conversations the Church Forgot. Baker Publishing Group, 2018.
5. https://biblehub.com/greek/5293.htm

11. The Question

1. https://biblehub.com/greek/5562.htm
2. https://biblehub.com/greek/2135.htm
3. https://biblehub.com/greek/1410.htm

12. Waiting For The Right Time

1. "Idle | Definition of Idle in English by Oxford Dictionaries." *Oxford Dictionaries | English*, Oxford Dictionaries, en.oxforddictionaries.com/definition/idle.
2. "Idle." *Merriam-Webster*, Merriam-Webster, www.merriam-webster.com/dictionary/idle.
3. https://biblehub.com/hebrew/6822.htm

13. Preparing For The Future

1. "Selfish." *Merriam-Webster*, Merriam-Webster, www.merriam-webster.com/dictionary/selfish.

14. Breaking Barriers

1. Lamia, Mary C. "Shame: A Concealed, Contagious, and Dangerous Emotion." *Psychology Today*, Sussex Publishers, www.psychologytoday.com/us/blog/intense-emotions-and-strong-feelings/201104/shame-concealed-contagious-and-dangerous-emotion.
2. Gardner, Tim Alan. Sacred Sex: a Spiritual Celebration of Oneness in Marriage. Waterbrook Press, 2003
3. https://biblehub.com/greek/5563.htm
4. Merriam-webster.com. (2019). *Definition of UNCONDITIONALLY*. [online] Available at: https://www.merriam-webster.com/dictionary/unconditionally [Accessed 17 Mar. 2019].

15. How You Think About Singleness

1. Gaultiere, Bill. "Jesus' Solitude and Silence." *Soul Shepherding*, 18 Sept. 2017, www.soulshepherding.org/jesus-solitude-and-silence/.
2. Meyer, Joyce, and Joyce Meyer. Battlefield of the Mind: Winning the Battle in Your Mind. Faith Words, 2017.

16. He Hasn't Forgotten You

1. 36. https://biblehub.com/hebrew/2710.htm

17. Why Am I Still Single?

1. transformed-https://biblehub.com/greek/3339.htm

Also by Hannah L M

Prayers For Your Future Husband

Made in the USA
Columbia, SC
05 January 2020